The Pock

MW00465120

Green Depression Era Glass

Monica Lynn Clements and Patricia Rosser Clements

4880 Lower Valley Road, Atglen, PA 19310 USA

Acknowledgments

Our special thanks to each of the contributors: Sharon Ainsworth, Joann Askew, Beth Horn, Denise Kaniss, Sara Lee, Margaret McRaney, Mary G. Moon, Craig and Paula Paige, 5-Paige Collectibles, Donna Stotts, Butterflies in the Attic, J. Marie Taylor, Jon Marc Taylor, Three Rivers Antiques of Jefferson, Texas, Yesterday's Antique Mall of Atlanta, Texas, and Pat Henry of Yesterday's Rose.

Published by Schiffer Publishing Ltd.
4880 Lower Valley Road
Atglen, PA 19310
Phone: (610) 593-1777; Fax: (610) 593-2002
E-mail: Schifferbk@aol.com
Please visit our web site catalog at **www.schifferbooks.com**
We are always looking for people to write books on new and related subjects. If you have an idea for a book, please contact us at the above address.

This book may be purchased from the publisher.
Include $3.95 for shipping.
Please try your bookstore first.
You may write for a free catalog.

In Europe, Schiffer books are distributed by
Bushwood Books
6 Marksbury Avenue
Kew Gardens
Surrey TW9 4JF England
Phone: 44 (0) 20 8392 8585
Fax: 44 (0) 20 8392 9876
E-mail: Bushwd@aol.com
Free postage in the UK. Europe: air mail at cost.

Copyright © 2002 by Monica Lynn Clements and Patricia Rosser Clements
Library of Congress Control Number: 2001095658

All rights reserved. No part of this work may be reproduced or used in any form or by any means—graphic, electronic, or mechanical, including photocopying or information storage and retrieval systems—without written permission from the copyright holder.
"Schiffer," "Schiffer Publishing Ltd. & Design," and the "Design of pen and ink well" are registered trademarks of Schiffer Publishing Ltd.

Designed by John P. Cheek
Cover design by Bruce M. Waters
Type set in University Roman Bd BT/Souvenir Lt BT

ISBN: 0-7643-1535-8
Printed in China
1 2 3 4

Contents

Introduction

The term *depression glass* originated in the 1970s as a way to identify glass made inexpensively during the years of the Great Depression. The meaning of this term has widened extensively, but for the purposes of this book, we have concentrated on the glass made from the late 1920s into the 1940s. Along with the traditional patterns, other pieces produced during the Depression Era are included in the last chapter. Among this glass are examples of elegant glassware.

At one time, Depression Era glass was plentiful. Today, the glass in every color has become scarce or very expensive. Therefore, many collectors look to reproductions to complete their sets or as pieces to use until they can locate the original pieces.

An extremely popular color in Depression Era glass, green glass in all patterns has become highly collectible. We hope you will enjoy the beauty of green Depression Era glass.

The purpose of this book is not to set prices but to be used as a guide.

Chapter One

History

The Great Depression

The Depression Era refers to the time in American history from 1929 to 1940. The Great Depression officially began on October 24, 1929, known as Black Tuesday, when the stock market collapsed. The result was financial ruin and panic that ran rampant.

Failed businesses and banks along with widespread unemployment devastated the economy for many years. The value of money had fallen and the need for goods declined. Perhaps the hardest hit were the farmers since there was no demand for what they produced. The mainstay of agriculture was demolished by the drought of the 1930s and the tragedy of the Great Plains Dust Bowl.

When Franklin Delano Roosevelt became president, the situation began to change. He came up with the idea for the New Deal and formed agencies to provide ways to help people out of their poverty. While Roosevelt's ideas changed people's lives and ensured that such a catastrophe would never happen again, it wasn't until World War II, with the need for new industry, that the problems caused by the Great Depression were solved completely.

Depression Era Glassware

In order to survive during the years of the Great Depression, glass companies turned to machines and came up with a way to mass produce glassware. The inexpensive formula for the glass included lime, silica, and soda ash.

Glass companies discovered several methods by which they produced Depression Era glass: chipped-mold, paste-mold, cut-mold, and mold-etched glass. Of these, the most popular and the most common way of fashioning glass was the chipped-mold method. This process involved a workman taking an iron mold and etching the design into the mold. After the glass had been placed into the mold, the result was a raised pattern. An advantage to using the chipped-mold method was that the raised design often hid the flaws of bubbles in the glass.

During the Depression Era, the companies which offered lines considered as elegant glass now turned to providing new items for American tables. For example, breakfast sets, bridge sets, luncheon sets, and other pieces such as the sandwich tray became common.

Companies worked to market the inexpensive glass through premiums and promotions. For example, buying a box of oatmeal or cornflakes could ensure that there would be a dish inside the box. Going to the movies could also provide a way to win glassware through a drawing. Other avenues for offering glass included magazine subscriptions.

Out of the array of colors available to consumers in the Depression Era patterns, green was one of the most popular. Companies offered patterns that contained green pieces.

Today, the green pieces are quite popular. Many collectors continue to add to collections although good pieces are more difficult to find and sometimes rather expensive.

Depression Era Glass Companies

Anchor Hocking Glass Company

What began as the Hocking Glass Company in the early 1900s became the Anchor Hocking Glass Company in 1937. The merging of Anchor Cap and Closure Corporation, its subsidiaries, and the Hocking Glass Company heralded the beginning of a strong force in the production of glassware.

With plants in Canada, New Jersey, New York, and Pennsylvania, the company continued to expand its base through the acquisition of Maywood Glass Company and the Carr-Lowrey Glass Company in the 1940s. Through these companies, Anchor Hocking entered into toiletries and cosmetic containers production.

Anchor Hocking continued with its wide ranging production of glassware that began during the Hocking Glass Company years. The company still produces glassware of durable quality. The Manhattan pattern and Oyster and Pearl pattern are representative of Anchor Hocking's top notch glassware production.

Fast becoming an important collectible line of glassware, Anchor Hocking's Fire-King creations exist in a wide array of shapes and patterns. The Fire-King line first appeared in the early 1940s and dinnerware, kitchenware, and ovenware were produced until the late 1970s. Anchor Hocking manufactured items that commemorated Fire-King's 50th anniversary in 1992. The Alice pattern, Jane Ray pattern, and Shell pattern were made in Jade-ite dinnerware. Many pieces were made in durable restaurant ware and kitchenware in Jade-ite.

Federal Glass Company

Located in Columbus, Ohio, the Federal Glass Company was considered an innovative company that thrived into the late 1970s. The manufacture of affordable glassware began in the early 1900s. Like other companies, Federal Glass Company created patterns using the old fashioned method of hand press-

Georgian Lovebirds by Federal.

ing. With the demand of consumers, the company turned to machines and soon made colored glass using machine pressed methods.

The mold-etched method was used to create such patterns in the color green as Georgian, Parrot, Patrician, and Sharon. During the 1930s, the company utilized the chip-mold method in the creation of Rosemary and Sharon. Colonial Fluted represents another successful pressed pattern that came from the company.

Georgian Lovebirds by Federal.

Madrid by Federal.

Thumbprint by Federal.

Patrician by Federal.

Colonial Fluted Rope by Federal.

Colonial Fluted Rope by Federal.

Optic Paneled by Federal.

Fenton Glass Company

Two brothers, Frank Fenton and John Fenton, founded Fenton Glass Company, which first appeared in 1906. Famous for its production of carnival glass during the 1920s, the company expanded its designs and began to produce patterns in an array of colors. In 1928, Fenton Glass Company introduced Lincoln Inn, a prominent and popular pattern found in green.

The success of Fenton Art Glass Company continues today in Williamstown, West Virginia. The family run firm produces fine glass that collectors enjoy in the present day.

Hazel-Atlas Glass Company

One of the most prolific companies that produced glass during the Depression Era was the Hazel-Atlas Glass Company. Perhaps this was due to the fact

Crisscross by Hazel-Atlas.

that the company operated several plants in Oklahoma, Pennsylvania, and West Virginia. In these plants, the company started its production by making containers and fruit jars. During the early 1900s, the West Virginia plant at Clarksburg became the central location where the manufacture of tableware began.

The myriad of patterns of Depression Era glass produced by Hazel-Atlas in green includes Aurora, Cloverleaf, Colonial Black, Florentine No. 1, Florentine No. 2, Fruits, Moderntone Platonite, New Century, Ribbon, and Royal Lace. Kitchenware items and a wide selection of glasses, pitchers, and the like also came from Hazel-Atlas.

Cloverleaf by Hazel-Atlas.

Colonial Block by Hazel-Atlas.

Colonial Block by Hazel-Atlas.

Colonial Block by Hazel-Atlas.

Florentine by Hazel-Atlas.

Florentine I by Hazel-Atlas.

New Century by Hazel-Atlas.

Ovide by Hazel-Atlas

New Century by Hazel-Atlas.

Ribbon by Hazel-Atlas.

Royal Lace by Hazel-Atlas.

Hocking Glass Company

Issac J. Collins was the mastermind behind the Hocking Glass Company. He assembled eight investors and enlisted the help of E. B. Good to purchase a glass company in Lancaster, Ohio. The company was renamed Hocking Glass Company because of its close proximity to the Hocking River.

With fifty employees, the Hocking Glass Company began its operation in 1905. Under Collins, the company flourished. A fire destroyed the company in 1924, and instead of signaling the end of the company, a new factory was built. The new factory devoted itself to the production of glassware. Six months after the fire, Hocking Glass Company was stronger than ever, having obtained controlling interest in two companies: the Lancaster Glass Company and the Standard Glass Manufacturing Company.

During the 1920s, Hocking became known for its innovative production of glassware through the use of technology. Their creation was a machine that had fifteen molds and manufactured ninety pieces of glass a minute. This innovation allowed Hocking Glass Company to thrive during a time when other companies struggled to stay in business or failed.

Hocking Glass Company items are in abundance today. In the mid 1920s, the company began producing green glass in occasional pieces. The number of important patterns in Depression Era glass was evidence that the company was prolific in glassware manufacture. Block Optic, Cameo, Circle, Colonial, Coronation, Fire-King Philbe, Mayfair, Miss America, Princess, Roulette, and Spiral, are patterns found in green.

Block Optic by Hocking.

Block Optic by Hocking.

Block Optic by Hocking.

Block Optic by Hocking.

Bubble by Hocking.

Above and below: Cameo by Hocking.

Cameo by Hocking.

Circle by Hocking.

Spiral by Hocking.

Spiral by Hocking.

Colonial ("Knife and Fork") by Hocking.

Colonial ("Knife and Fork") by Hocking.

Colonial ("Knife and Fork") by Hocking.

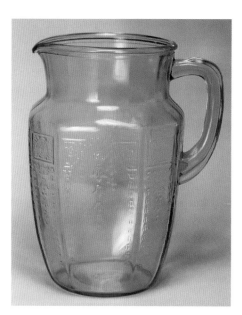

Princess by Hocking.

Princess by Hocking.

Ring by Hocking.

Roulette by Hocking.

Imperial Glass Corporation

A company associated with the making of iridescent glass was the Imperial Glass Corporation. This company's founder was Edward Muhleman. In 1904, the company began its manufacturing of glass and would continue for the next eighty years. During the 1930s, Imperial bought the molds from the Central Glass Company. Later, Imperial would purchase Heisey Company and Cambridge Glass Company.

Imperial produced a wide variety of designs in iridescent blown and pressed glass. The company dabbled in Depression Era glass patterns. Those patterns available in green are Beaded Block, Diamond Quilted (also known as "Flat Diamond"), and Twisted Optic.

Diamond Quilted ("Flat Diamond") by Imperial.

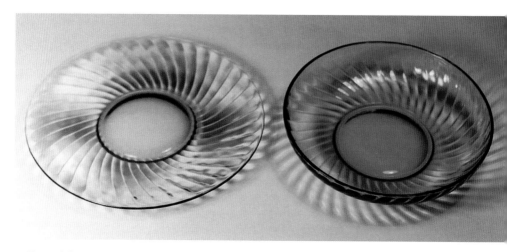

Twisted Optic by Imperial.

Bowl by Imperial.

Indiana Glass Company

Located in Dunkirk, Indiana, the Indiana Glass Company began in 1904 and continues to produce glass in the present day. Early advertisements from the company boasted its manufacture of goblets, lamps, soda fountain supplies, and tableware. During the 1920s and 1930s, the company produced several Depression Era patterns. The durable and distinctive Tea Room was produced in the color green.

Daisy by Indiana.

Lorain ("Basket") No. 615 by Indiana.

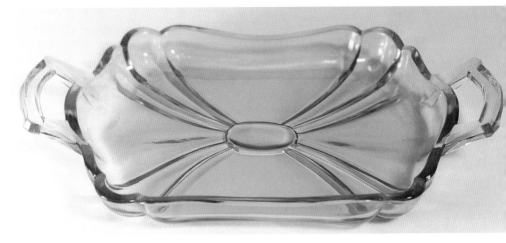

Bananas, No. 611 by Indiana.

Avocado
by
Indiana.

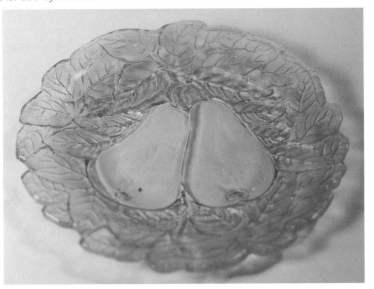

Avocado by Indiana.

Horseshoe by Indiana.

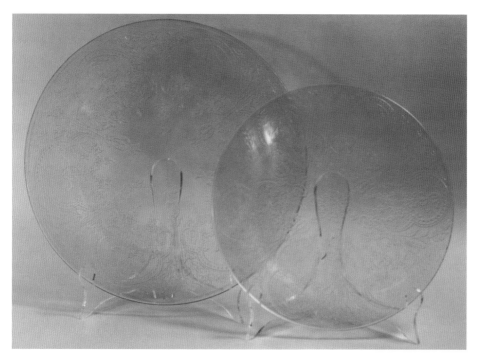

Horseshoe by Indiana.

Old English by Indiana.

Pyramid by Indiana.

Tea Room by Indiana.

Jeannette Glass Company

The Jeannette Glass Company originated in the late 1890s. By the 1920s, the company had turned to machinery for production of its glassware. Through the years, Jeannette Glass Company manufactured tableware, novelty items, candy containers, and kitchenware. For many years, the main colors of glass coming from this company were pink and green.

"Jeannette Green," a green similar to apple green, was introduced in 1925. The opaque jade green known as Jade-ite was introduced in 1932. The pressed patterns remained favorites with Cube (also know as "Cubist"), Sierra, and Windsor (Windsor Diamond). The company followed with etched glass patterns such as Cherry Blossom and Floral.

Cube ("Cubist") by Jeannette.

Floral by Jeanette.

Sierra by Jeannette.

Windsor by Jeannette.

Windsor by Jeannette.

Windsor by Jeannette.

Cherry Blossom by Jeannette.

Doric by Jeannette.

Doric by Jeannette.

Tumblers by Jeannette.

Lancaster Glass Company

In the early 1900s, the father and son team of Lucien B. Martin and L. Phillip Martin started the Lancaster Glass Company in Lancaster, Ohio. The company began producing fine vases in 1909 and from there moved into the manufacture of tableware and novelties, including animal figures.

The Lancaster Glass Company produced stylish patterns of green Depression Era glass during the 1930s. Etched patterns such as Sphinx share the same shape as other patterns.

Macbeth-Evans Glass Company

During the years of the Depression, the Macbeth-Evans Company produced green glass. The glassware made by this company was often thinner and more delicate than the glass of patterns made by other companies. Unlike other companies, the Macbeth-Evans Company did not manufacture such items as butter dishes, candlesticks, or cookie jars.

In the late 1920s, the company began its Depression Era patterns with the mold-etched pattern Dogwood (also called "Apple Blossom" or "Wild Rose"). Another green pattern was Thistle. The same mold was used for the production of both patterns.

U. S. Glass Company

The United States Glass Company consolidated fifteen glass factories as a way to produce glass in a more efficient way and eliminate competition. Thus, the company began in 1891 to manufacture all kinds of glass items from soda glasses to tableware to novelty items and more.

The zenith of the company's glass production came between 1920 and 1940. Glass in a wide array of colors and styles was created, with the company achieving success with its lines of iridescent glass as well as satin glass. Like other glass companies, U. S. Glass Company manufactured inexpensive glass in different colors.

In the 1920s, the company produced many of their lines in green. Patterns in green from this company were Cherryberry, Floral and Diamond Band, Flower Garden with Butterflies (also called "Butterflies and Roses"), Strawberry, and U. S. Swirl.

Floral and Diamond Band by U. S. Glass.

Octagon by U. S. Glass.

Shaggy Daisy by U. S. Glass.

Rose and Thorn by U. S. Glass.

Westmoreland Glass Company

First known for its novelty items and condiments, the Westmoreland Glass Company located in Grapeville, Pennsylvania, originated in 1890. The company's creations in candy dishes and the like could be found in dime stores, but by the 1920s, the company decided to specialize in glassware. Westmoreland took its glass making seriously and soon had the largest factory where the production and decoration of glass took place.

English Hobnail, a hand molded pattern, with its characteristic bumps proved a popular design. This pattern was produced in green from 1925 until the 1930s.

Chapter Two

Depression Era Patterns

Adam

Made by the Jeannette Glass Company from 1932 to 1934.

Bowl, 4.75"	$22-25
Bowl, 7.74"	$27-30
Bowl, cereal, 5.75"	$50-55
Bowl, oval vegetable, 10"	$35-40
Butter dish and cover	$385-400
Creamer, 3"	$25-30
Cup	$25-30
Plate, sherbet, 6"	$10-12
Plate, square salad, 7.75"	$18-22
Plate, dinner, 9"	$30-36
Platter, 11.75"	$32-35
Saucer	$6-7
Sherbet	$36-38
Sugar with cover	$65-75

American Pioneer

Made by Liberty Works from 1931 to 1934.

Bowl, handled, 5"	$27-28
Bowl, handled, 9"	$28-31
Bowl, 10"	$68-72
Creamer	$30-33
Cup	$11-13
Goblet, 8 oz.	$44-47
Plate, 6"	$17-19
Plate, 8"	$12-15
Saucer	$5-7
Sugar, 2.75" high	$26-28
Sugar, 3.5" high	$26-28
Tumbler, 8 oz.	$54-56
Tumbler, 12 oz.	$54-56

Avocado, or No. 601

Made by the Indiana Glass Company from 1923 to 1933.

Bowl, salad, 7.5"	$65-70
Bowl, oval, two handles, 9"	$32-35
Creamer, 3.75"	$38-40
Cup, footed	$40-42
Plate, 6.25"	$20-28
Plate, salad, 8.25"	$22-28
Saucer	$24-25
Sugar, 3"	$38-40

Block Optic ("Block")

Made by the Hocking Glass Company from 1929 to 1933.

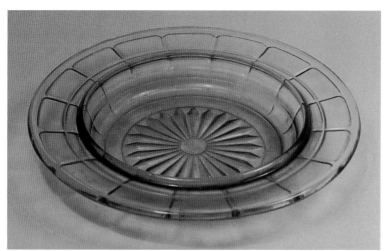

Bowl, 4.25"	$9-12
Bowl, cereal, 5.25"	$15-18
Bowl, salad, 7.25"	$170-175
Bowl, berry, 8.5"	$30-35
Butter dish, 3" x 5"	$50-75
Candy jar w/lid, 2.25" high	$60-65
Creamer	$13-14
Cup	$7-8
Goblet, cocktail, 4"	$40-45
Goblet, wine, 4.5"	$40-45
Goblet, 5.75"	$27-35
Ice bucket	$45-60
Plate, sherbet, 6"	$3-4

Plate, salad, 8"	$6-7
Plate, dinner, 9"	$25-30
Salt and pepper, footed	$42-43
Salt and pepper	$99-102
Saucer	$8-10
Sherbet, cone, no stem	$4-8
Sherbet, 3.25"	$6-9
Sherbet, 4.75"	$18-20
Tumbler, flat, 9.5 oz., 3.75"	$15-18
Tumbler, flat, 10 oz.	$22-25

Bowknot

Manufacturer unknown. Probably made in the late 1920s.

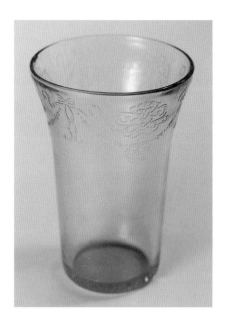

Bowl, cereal, 5.5"	$30-35
Cup	$9-11
Plate, salad, 7"	$14-15
Sherbet	$18-20
Tumbler, flat, 5"	$25-28
Tumbler, with foot, 5"	$20-25

Bubble

Made by the Hocking Glass Company from 1937 to 1965.

Bowl, vegetable, 8.25"	$15-25
Creamer	$14-15
Cup	$8-9
Plate, salad, 6.75"	$5-12
Plate, dinner, 9.25"	$28-30
Plate, dinner, 9.75"	$20-40
Saucer	$3-5
Sugar	$13-14

Cameo ("Ballerina" or "Dancing Girl")

Made by the Hocking Glass Company from 1930 to 1934.

Bowl, cereal, 5.5"	$33-35
Bowl, salad, 7.25"	$60-75
Bowl, soup, 9"	$75-100
Bowl, vegetable oval, 10"	$35-45
Butter dish with lid	$235-250
Cake plate, with three feet, 10"	$25-40
Creamer, 3.25"	$24-25
Creamer, 4.25"	$28-30
Cup	$12-15
Goblet, water, 5.75"	$62-65
Pitcher, water, 8.5"	$60-75
Plate, sherbet, 6"	$5-6
Plate, luncheon, 8.25"	$12-14
Plate, dinner, 9.5"	$22-25
Plate, sandwich, 10"	$18-20
Sherbet, with stem, 4.88"	$35-38
Sugar, 3.25"	$22-25
Sugar, 4.25"	$28-30
Tumbler, water, 4"	$30-40
Tumbler, 5.25"	$80-90

Cherry Blossom

Made by the Jeannette Glass Company from 1930 to 1939.

Bowl, cereal, 5.75"	$48-50
Bowl, flat soup, 7.75"	$90-95
Bowl, berry, 8.5"	$50-55
Bowl, oval vegetable, 9"	$45-55
Bowl, footed fruit, 10.5"	$95-100
Butter dish	$110-120
Cake plate, 10.25"	$38-45
Coaster, 3.25"	$14-18
Creamer	$22-24
Cup	$22-23
Plate, sherbet, 6"	$10-12
Plate, salad, 7"	$24-30
Plate, dinner, 9"	$27-30
Platter, oval, 11"	$55-60
Saucer	$5-6
Sherbet, 2.75"	$22-28
Sugar with lid	$18-38
Tray, handled, 10.5"	$33-45
Tumbler, footed, 3.75"	$22-25

Note: During the 1970s, reproduction dishes began to appear on the market.

Circle

Made by the Hocking Glass Company during the 1930s.

Bowl, 4.5"	$8-12
Bowl, 5"	$12-16
Bowl, 8"	$18-30
Bowl, 9.25"	$25-30
Creamer	$10-12
Cup	$5-6
Goblet, wine, 4.5"	$13-15
Goblet, water, 8 oz.	$11-15
Pitcher, 60 oz.	$60-75
Plate, sherbet, 6"	$2-5
Plate, luncheon, 8.25"	$4-8
Plate, luncheon, 9.5"	$6-8
Plate, dinner, 9.5"	$38-40
Plate, sandwich, 10"	$14-15
Saucer	$2-8
Sherbet, with stem, 3.12"	$4-8
Sherbet, with stem, 4.75"	$6-10
Sugar	$10-12
Tumbler, juice, 3.5"	$8-12

Tumbler, water, 4"	$9-10
Tumbler, iced tea, 5"	$16-18
Tumbler, 15 oz.	$22-25

Cloverleaf

Made by the Hazel-Atlas Glass Company from 1930 to 1936.

Ashtray, 4"	$63-65
Ashtray, 5.75"	$85-90
Bowl, dessert, 4"	$30-35
Bowl, salad, 7"	$50-55
Bowl, 8"	$80-85
Creamer	$10-15
Cup	$9-10
Plate, sherbet, 6"	$6-8
Plate, luncheon, 8"	$8-10
Saucer	$3-5
Sugar	$10-15
Tumbler, flat, 3.75"	$60-75
Tumbler, footed, 5.75"	$28-35

Colonial ("Knife and Fork")

Made by the Hocking Glass Company from 1934 to 1938.

Bowl, berry, 4.5"	$18-20
Bowl, cream soup, 4.5"	$70-75
Bowl, cereal, 5.5"	$100-110
Bowl, low soup, 7"	$65-70
Bowl, berry, 9"	$30-35
Butter dish with lid	$55-60
Creamer, 5"	$25-35
Cup	$12-14
Goblet, cordial, 3.75"	$25-30
Goblet, cocktail, 4"	$25-28
Goblet, wine, 4.5"	$25-28
Goblet, claret, 5.25"	$25-28
Goblet, water, 5.75"	$32-33
Pitcher, 68 oz. 7.75"	$80-85
Plate, sherbet or saucer, 6"	$8-9
Plate, luncheon, 8.5"	$10-11
Plate, dinner, 10"	$65-70
Platter, oval, 12"	$25-35
Salt and pepper	$150-160
Sherbet,	$12-15
Sugar bowl with lid	$45-48
Tumbler, flat water, 4"	$22-25
Tumbler, footed, 4"	$44-45

Colonial Block

Made by the Hazel-Atlas Glass Company from the late 1920s until the early 1930s.

Bowl, 4"	$8-10
Bowl, 7"	$20-22
Butter dish with lid	$40-45
Butter tub	$45-60
Creamer	$12-15
Goblet	$13-15
Pitcher	$45-75
Sherbet	$8-10
Sugar with lid	$20-30
Tumbler, footed, 5.25"	$30-55

Colonial Fluted ("Rope")

Made by Federal Glass Company from 1928 to 1933.

Bowl, 4"	$10-12
Bowl, 6"	$13-16
Cup	$7-9
Plate, 6"	$3-5
Plate, 8"	$5-8
Sherbet	$6-9

Cube ("Cubist")

Made by the Jeannette Glass Company from 1929 to 1933.

Bowl, dessert, 4.5"	$7-10
Bowl, salad, 6.5"	$15-22
Butter dish with lid	$65-100
Candy jar with lid	$33-55
Creamer 3.25"	$10-12
Cup	$9-12
Pitcher, 8.75"	$235-260
Plate, sherbet, 6"	$4-10
Plate, luncheon, 8"	$11-15
Powder jar with lid, three feet	$33-40
Saucer	$3-4
Sherbet	$11-12
Sugar base, 3"	$8-12
Sugar or candy lid	$15-22
Tumbler, 4"	$78-90

Daisy, No. 620

Made by the Indiana Glass Company from late 1930 to 1980. Made in green from 1960-1980.

Berry Bowl, 4.5"	$6-7
Berry Bowl, 7.33"	$9-11
Berry Bowl, 9.33"	$14-15
Cereal Bowl, 6"	$10-11
Creamer	$7-9
Cup	$5-7
Plate, luncheon, 8.33"	$5-7
Plate, Dinner, 9.33"	$7-9
Saucer	$2-3
Vegetable Bowl, oval, 10"	$10-12

Diamond Quilted ("Flat Diamond")

Made by the Imperial Glass Company from the late 1920s to the early 1930s.

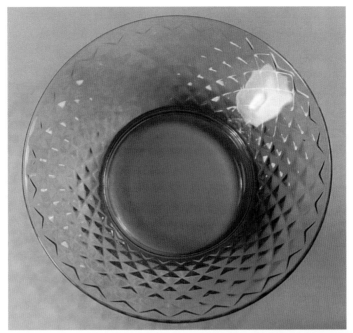

Bowl, cream soup	$10-20
Bowl, with one handle, 5.5"	$10-22
Bowl, crimped edge, 7"	$9-18
Bowl, rolled edge, console, 10.5"	$20-30
Candy jar, footed, with lid	$65-125
Compote, with lid, 11.25"	$95-120
Creamer	$10-12
Cup	$9-10
Plate, sherbet, 6.5"	$4-8
Plate, salad, 7"	$6-10
Plate, luncheon, 8"	$6-12
Plate, sandwich, 14"	$15-20
Punch bowl and stand	$495-500
Sandwich server w/ center handle	$25-30
Saucer	$4-5
Sherbet, 3.5"	$9-10
Tumbler, footed, 6 oz.	$8-10
Tumbler, water, flat or footed, 9 oz.	$9-15

Doric

Made by the Jeannette Glass Company from 1935 to 1938.

Bowl, berry, 4.5"	$11-12
Bowl, cream soup, 5"	$450-500
Bowl, cereal, 5.5"	$85-100
Bowl, berry, 8.25"	$32-35
Bowl, with two handles, 9"	$22-25
Bowl, oval vegetable, 9"	$40-45
Butter dish with lid	$85-100
Cake plate, with three legs	$28-30
Candy dish, divided	$12-15
Candy jar, with lid, 8"	$40-42
Coaster, 3"	$18-20
Creamer	$14-18
Cup	$10-12
Pitcher, footed, 7.5"	$1150-1200
Plate, sherbet, 6"	$7-8
Plate, salad, 7"	$25-28
Plate, dinner, 9"	$19-25
Platter, oval, 12"	$30-35
Relish tray, 4" x 4"	$8-10
Relish tray, 4" x 8"	$18-20
Salt and pepper	$37-40
Saucer	$4-5
Sherbet	$17-18
Sugar with lid	$42-50
Tray, 8" x 8"	$30-40
Tumbler, flat, 4.5"	$110-120
Tumbler, footed, 5"	$125-150

English Hobnail

Made by the Westmoreland Glass Company from the 1920s to 1940s.

Ashtray, 3"	$18-20
Bowl, round nappy, 6"	$17-18
Bowl, grapefruit, 6.5"	$20-25
Bowl, celery, 12"	$35-40
Candy dish w/ lid and three feet, 6"	$60-70
Candy jar with lid, cone shape	$55-65
Creamer, flat or footed	$22-50
Cup	$18-20
Cup and saucer, demitasse	$60-65
Marmalade with cover	$40-50
Pitcher, 23 oz.	$145-150
Plate, sherbet, 5.5"	$8-10
Plate, 6.5"	$8-10
Plate, 8"	$12-14
Plate 10"	$32-40
Salt and pepper	$77-85
Saucer	$4-5
Sugar	$24-25
Tumbler, iced tea, 12 oz.	$30-33

Fire-King Dinnerware "Alice"

Made by the Anchor Hocking Company in the 1940s.

Cup	$7-8
Plate	$28-32
Saucer	$3-4

WE HOPE THAT YOU ENJOY THIS BOOK...and that it will occupy a proud place in your library. We would like to keep you informed about other publications from Schiffer Books. Please return this card with your requests and comments.

Title of Book Purchased _____

☐ Purchased at: _____ ☐ received as a gift

Comments or ideas for books you would like to see us publish: _____

Your Name: _____

Address _____

City _____ State _____ Zip _____

E-mail Address _____

☐ Please send me a **free** *Schiffer Antiques, Collectibles, Arts and Design Catalog*
☐ Please send me a **free** *Schiffer Woodcarving, Woodworking, and Crafts Catalog*
☐ Please send me a **free** *Schiffer Military, Aviation, and Automotive History Catalog*
☐ Please send me a **free** *Whitford Body, Mind, and Spirit Catalog*
☐ Please send me information about new releases via email.
  We don't share our mailing list with anyone

See our most current books on the web at **www.schifferbooks.com**

Contact us at: Phone: 610-593-1777; Fax: 610-593-2002; or E-mail: schifferbk@aol.com
SCHIFFER BOOKS ARE CURRENTLY AVAILABLE FROM YOUR BOOKSELLER

K: userido\wp\basic\bouceback

SCHIFFER PUBLISHING LTD
4880 LOWER VALLEY ROAD
ATGLEN, PA 19310-9717 USA

PLACE
STAMP
HERE

Fire-King Dinnerware "Jane-Ray"

Made by the Anchor Hocking Company from 1945 to the 1960s.

Bowl, dessert, 4.88"	$9-11
Bowl, oatmeal, 5.88"	$18-22
Bowl, soup, 7.62"	$23-26
Bowl, vegetable, 8.25"	$25-27
Cup	$6-7
Creamer	$8-11
Plate, salad, 7.75"	$12-13
Plate, dinner, 9.12"	$14-16
Platter, 12"	$24-26
Saucer	$3-4
Sugar	$9-11
Sugar cover	$22-24

Floral ("Poinsettia")

Made by the Jeannette Glass Company from 1931 to 1935.

Creamer	$18-22
Cup	$14-15
Pitcher, footed, 8"	$42-45
Plate, sherbet, 6"	$9-10
Plate, salad, 8"	$15-16
Plate, dinner, 9"	$20-22
Saucer	$10-12
Sherbet	$20-22
Sugar	$12-18
Sugar cover	$20-30
Tumbler, footed water, 4.75"	$24-30
Tumbler, footed lemonade, 5.25"	$60-65

Floral and Diamond Band

Made by the U. S. Glass Company from 1927 to 1931.

Bowl, berry, 4.5"	$10-12
Bowl, large berry, 8"	$18-20
Butter dish and cover	$130-150
Creamer, 4.75"	$18-20
Pitcher, 42 oz., 8"	$120-125
Plate, luncheon, 8"	$45-55
Sherbet	$8-10
Sugar, 5.25"	$18-20
Sugar lid	$65-70
Tumbler, water, 4"	$25-30
Tumbler, iced tea, 5"	$50-65

Florentine No. 1 ("Poppy No. 1")

Made by the Hazel-Atlas Glass Company from 1923 to 1936.

Bowl, berry, 5"	$12-20
Bowl, cereal, 6"	$25-40
Berry bowl, large, 8.5"	$25-45
Butter with cover	$125-140
Creamer, 3"	$8-10
Creamer, ruffled	$42-45
Pitcher, footed, 36 oz., 6.5"	$45-50
Plate, grill, 10"	$12-20
Platter, oval, 11.5"	$20-30
Salt and pepper	$37-50
Sherbet	$11-15
Sugar with cover	$28-35

Georgian ("Lovebirds")

Made by the Federal Glass Company from 1931 to 1936.

Bowl, berry, 4.5"	$10-12
Bowl, cereal, 5.75"	$22-25
Bowl, large berry, 7.5"	$63-70
Bowl, oval vegetable, 9"	$63-60
Butter dish and cover	$75-85
Cup	$10-12
Plate, sherbet, 6"	$7-10
Plate, luncheon, 8"	$10-12

Plate, dinner, 9.25"	$25-40
Saucer	$3-8
Sherbet	$12-15
Sugar base, 3"	$10-14
Sugar lid, for 3" base	$45-50
Tumbler, flat, 9 oz., 4"	$65-80
Tumbler, flat, 12 oz., 5.25"	$135-150

Horseshoe

Made by the Indiana Glass Company from 1930 to 1933.

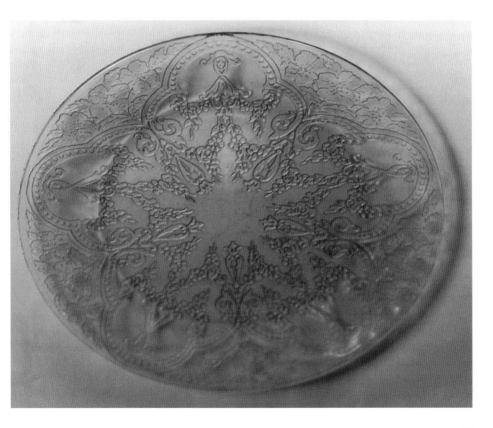

Bowl, berry, 4.5"	$28-30
Bowl, cereal, 6.5"	$30-35
Bowl, salad, 7.5"	$25-30
Bowl, 9.5"	$45-50
Bowl, oval vegetable, 10.5"	$30-40
Creamer	$18-20
Plate, sherbet, 6"	$10-16
Plate, salad, 8.25"	$12-15
Plate, luncheon, 9.5"	$14-15
Plate, sandwich, 11.5"	$22-25
Relish, three part	$25-30
Saucer	$5-10
Sherbet	$16-18
Sugar	$18-20
Tumbler, footed, 9 oz., 5.75"	$25-30

Lorain ("Basket"), No. 615

Made by the Indiana Glass Company from 1929 to 1932.

Bowl, cereal, 6"	$48-60
Bowl, salad, 7.25"	$48-50
Bowl, deep berry, 8"	$110-120
Creamer	$18-20
Cup	$11-15
Plate, sherbet, 5.5"	$8-10
Plate, salad, 7.75"	$10-15
Plate, dinner, 10.25"	$48-75
Platter, 11.5"	$33-35
Saucer	$4-7
Sherbet, footed	$25-28
Sugar, footed	$18-20

Madrid

Made by the Federal Glass Company from 1932 to 1939

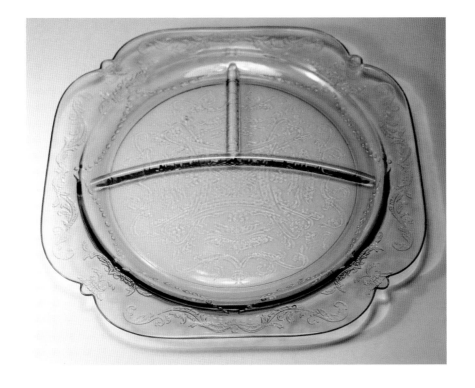

Bowl, oval vegetable, 10"	$22-30
Cup	$8-10
Hot dish coaster	$50-155
Plate, sherbet, 6"	$4-7
Plate, salad, 7.5"	$15-20
Plate, grill, 10.5"	$16-20
Plate, relish, 10.25"	$16-25
Platter, oval	$16-25
Saucer	$5-7
Sherbet	$11-12
Sugar	$12-20
Sugar lid	$60-65

Mount Pleasant ("Double Shield")

Made by the L. E. Smith Glass Company from the 1920s to 1934.

Bowl, mayonnaise, 5.5"	$20-30
Bowl, square handled, 6"	$18-20
Bowl, scalloped footed, 9"	$20-35
Bowl, scalloped, 10"	$35-42
Candlestick, double, each	$20-23
Creamer	$15-20
Cup	$10-14
Plate, handled mint, 6"	$20-25
Plate, scalloped, square, 8"	$10-18
Plate, two handles, 8"	$10-18
Plate, grill, 9"	$10-20
Plate, handled, 12"	$15-33
Sugar	$15-20

New Century

Made by the Hazel-Atlas Glass Company from 1930 to 1935.

Ashtray/coaster, 5.25"	$28-30
Bowl, berry, 4.5"	$25-35
Bowl, cream soup, 4.75"	$20-25
Bowl, large berry, 8"	$25-30
Creamer	$10-12
Cup	$6-10
Plate, sherbet, 6"	$5-7
Plate, salad, 8.5"	$12-13
Plate, dinner, 10"	$20-25
Platter, 11"	$22-30
Salt and pepper	$35-45
Saucer	$3-5
Sugar	$10-12
Sugar cover	$18-28
Tumbler, 5 oz., 3.5"	$12-15
Tumbler, 10 oz., 5"	$15-20
Tumbler, 12 oz., 5.25"	$28-30
Tumbler, footed, 5 oz., 4"	$20-30
Tumbler, footed, 9 oz., 4.75"	$22-30

Old English ("Threading")

Made by the Indiana Glass Company in the late 1920s.

Bowl, berry, 4"	$20-25
Bowl, footed fruit, 9"	$30-35
Bowl, flat, 9.5"	$40-50
Candlestick, pair, 4"	$40-60
Candy jar, footed with lid	$55-75
Creamer	$18-25
Pitcher	$70-80
Pitcher, with cover	$120-135
Sandwich server, center handle	$60-75
Sherbet, two styles	$22-25
Sugar base	$18-25
Sugar cover	$35-40

Ovide

Made by the Hazel Atlas Glass Company from 1930 to 1935.

Candy dish, with lid	$22-30
Cocktail, footed	$3-4
Creamer	$3-4
Cup	$3-4
Plate, sherbet, 6"	$2-3
Plate, luncheon, 8"	$3-4
Salt and pepper	$27-30
Saucer	$2-3
Sherbet	$2-3
Sugar	$4-5

Patrician ("Spoke")

Made by the Federal Glass Company from 1933 to 1937.

Bowl, cream soup 4.75"	$22-25
Bowl, berry, 5"	$12-15
Bowl, cereal, 6"	$28-30
Bowl, large berry, 8.5"	$40-45
Bowl, vegetable, 10"	$35-40
Butter with cover	$120-125
Creamer	$12-18
Cup	$12-13
Pitcher, molded handle, 8"	$145-150
Pitcher, applied handle, 8.25"	$170-175
Plate, bread and butter, 6"	$8-12
Plate, salad, 7.5"	$14-18
Plate, luncheon, 9"	$14-15
Plate, dinner, 10.5"	$42-45
Platter, 11.5"	$22-35
Saucer	$9-12
Sherbet	$15-18
Sugar with cover	$85-88

Princess

Made by the Hocking Glass Company from 1931 to 1935.

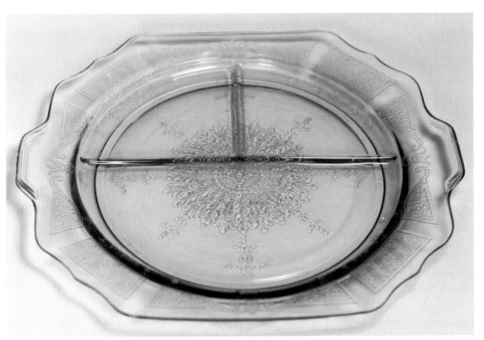

Ashtray, 4.5"	$75-85
Bowl, berry, 4.5"	$28-30
Bowl, cereal or oatmeal, 5.5"	$40-45
Bowl, salad, 9"	$42-65
Bowl, hat shaped, 9.5"	$55-80
Bowl, vegetable, 10"	$30-40
Butter with cover	$100-125
Candy jar with lid	$65-70
Coaster	$45-85
Creamer, oval	$18-20
Cup	$12-15
Pitcher, 37 oz., 6"	$58-70
Pitcher, footed, 24 oz., 7.5"	$550-750
Pitcher, 60 oz., 8"	$58-60
Plate, sherbet, 5.5"	$8-10
Plate, salad	$15-20
Plate, dinner, 9.5"	$25-30
Plate, grill, 9.5"	$15-16
Plate, sandwich, closed handles, 10.25"	$15-30
Platter, 12"	$28-30
Sherbet, footed	$20-25
Sugar with cover	$35-45

Pyramid, No. 610

Made by the Indiana Glass Company from 1928 to 1932.

Bowl, berry, 4.75"	$25-30
Bowl, berry, 8.5"	$45-60
Bowl, oval, 9.5"	$40-45
Creamer	$30-35
Ice tub	$125-145
Pitcher	$325-350
Relish tray, handled	$58-60
Sugar	$30-35
Tray for sugar and creamer	$25-30
Tumbler, footed, 8 oz.	$50-60
Tumbler, footed, 11 oz.	$75-80

Ribbon

Made by the Hazel Atlas Glass Company from 1930 to 1932.

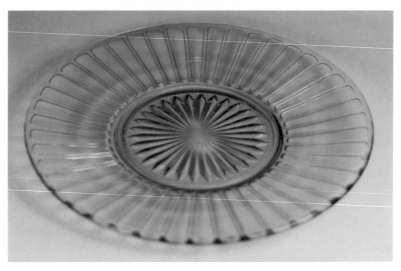

Bowl, berry, 4"	$30-40
Bowl, cereal, 5"	$38-40
Bowl, large berry, 8"	$38-40
Candy dish with cover	$40-42
Creamer, 3.5"	$15-18
Cup	$4-5
Plate, sherbet, 6.25"	$3-4
Plate, luncheon, 8"	$4-5
Salt and pepper	$30-35
Saucer	$2-3
Sherbet, 3"	$5-6
Sugar, 3.5"	$14-18
Tumbler, 5.5"	$30-33

Ring ("Banded Rings")

Made by the Hocking Glass Company from 1927 to 1932.

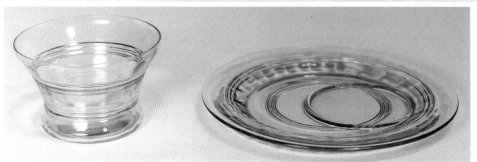

Bowl, berry, 5"	$5-6
Bowl, soup, 7"	$14-15
Bowl, 8"	$14-15
Creamer	$6-8
Cup	$5-6
Goblet, 9 oz., 7.25"	$13-15
Plate, sherbet, 6"	$2-5

Plate, sherbet, off center indent, 6.5"	$5-6
Plate, luncheon, 8"	$5-6
Sandwich server, open handle	$24-27
Saucer	$2-3
Sherbet, for 6.5" plate	$12-18
Sherbet, stemmed, 4.75"	$8-9
Sugar	$5-8
Tumbler, flat, 5 oz., 3.5"	$6-7
Tumbler, flat, 9 oz., 4.25"	$9-10
Tumbler, footed	$9-10

Rose Cameo

Made by the Belmont
Tumbler Company in
1931.

Bowl, berry, 4.5"	$12-15
Bowl, cereal, 5"	$18-20
Plate, salad	$14-18
Sherbet	$14-15
Tumbler, two styles, 5"	$23-25

Roulette ("Many Windows")

Made by the Hocking Glass Company from 1935 to 1939.

Bowl, fruit	$23-25
Cup	$7-8
Pitcher, 64 oz., 8"	$45-50
Plate, sherbet, 6"	$5-8
Plate, luncheon, 8.5"	$7-8
Plate, sandwich, 12"	$16-20
Saucer	$3-5
Sherbet	$7-8
Tumbler, old-fashioned, 7.5 oz., 3.25"	$43-45
Tumbler, juice, 5 oz., 3.5"	$25-35
Tumbler, water, 9 oz., 4.12"	$30-35
Tumbler, iced tea, 12 oz., 5.12"	$30-35
Tumbler, footed, 10 oz., 5.5"	$35-37

Round Robin

Made by an unknown manufacturer from 1927 to 1932.

Bowl, berry, 4"	$9-10
Creamer	$9-10
Cup	$5-7
Domino tray	$55-100
Plate, sherbet, 6"	$2-5
Plate, luncheon, 8"	$4-10
Plate, sandwich, 12"	$12-15
Saucer	$2-3
Sherbet	$9-10
Sugar	$9-10

Royal Lace

Made by the Hazel-Atlas Glass Company from 1934 to 1941.

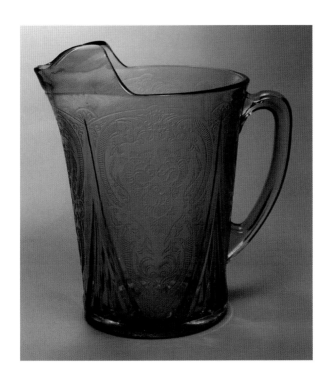

Bowl, cream soup, 4.75"	$35-40
Bowl, berry, 5"	$30-85
Bowl, round, 10"	$35-75
Bowl, oval vegetable, 11"	$35-85
Butter with cover	$275-450
Creamer	$25-45
Cup and saucer	$25-30
Pitcher, straight, 48 oz.	$110-150
Pitcher, with no ice lip, 64 oz., 8"	$110-225
Pitcher, 86 oz., 8"	$135-300
Pitcher, with ice lip, 96 oz., 8.5"	$140-275
Plate, sherbet, 6"	$12-15
Plate, luncheon, 8.5"	$18-40
Plate, dinner, 9.88"	$30-40
Platter, oval, 13"	$45-65
Salt and pepper	$130-200
Saucer	$14-15
Sherbet, footed	$25-45
Sugar	$25-45
Sugar lid	$40-80

Sharon ("Cabbage Rose")

Made by the Federal Glass Company from 1935 to 1939.

Bowl, berry, 5"	$18-19
Bowl, cereal, 6"	$30-32
Bowl, large berry, 8.5"	$38-40
Bowl, oval, 9.5"	$38-40
Bowl, fruit, 10.5"	$40-50
Cake plate, footed, 11.5"	$60-65
Candy jar with lid	$100-180
Creamer, footed	$22-25
Jam dish, 7.5"	$48-75
Plate, bread and butter, 6"	$9-10
Plate, salad, 7.5"	$20-25
Plate, dinner, 9.5"	$25-27
Platter, 12.5"	$30-35
Saucer	$15-20
Sherbet	$35-38
Sugar base	$20-25
Sugar cover	$45-55

Sierra ("Pinwheel")

Made by the Jeannette Glass Company from 1931 to 1933.

Bowl, cereal, 5.5"	$18-25
Bowl, berry 8.5"	$32-40
Bowl, oval vegetable, 9.25"	$125-175
Butter dish with cover	$50-70
Creamer	$23-28
Cup	$15-16
Pitcher, 6.5"	$140-150
Plate, dinner, 9"	$25-30
Platter, oval, 11"	$65-70
Salt and pepper	$45-60
Saucer	$9-10
Sugar base	$26-28
Sugar cover	$19-28
Tumbler, 4.5"	$85-90

Spiral

Made by the Hocking Glass Company from 1928 to 1930.

Bowl, berry, 4.75"	$5-7	Platter, 12"	$30-33
Bowl, mixing, 7"	$10-12	Salt and pepper	$35-80
Bowl, berry, 8"	$12-14	Saucer	$2-3
Creamer, flat or footed	$8-10	Sherbet	$4-5
Cup	$5-6	Sugar, flat or footed	$8-10
Ice bucket	$30-35	Tumbler, juice, 5 oz., 3"	$4-8
Pitcher, 58 oz., 7.66"	$35-45	Tumbler, water, 9 oz., 5"	$7-10
Plate, sherbet, 6"	$2-5	Tumbler, footed, 5.75"	$15-18
Plate, luncheon, 8"	$4-5	Vase, 5.75"	$47-50

Sunflower

Made by Jeannette Glass Company in the 1930s.

Cake plate, 10"	$15-17
Creamer	$19-21
Cup	$15-15
Plate, dinner, 9"	$19-21
Saucer	$13-14
Sugar	$22-24
Tumbler, footed, 8 oz., 4.33"	$34-36

Tea Room

Made by the Indiana Glass Company from 1926 to 1931.

Bowl, finger	$60-65
Bowl, banana split, 7.5"	$115-120
Bowl, celery, 8.5"	$30-35
Bowl, deep salad, 8.75"	$90-95.
Bowl, oval vegetable, 9.5"	$70-75
Candlestick, low, pair	$60-80
Cup	$55-60
Creamer, 4"	$22-26
Creamer and sugar on tray, 3.5"	$75-78
Goblet, 9 oz.	$75-85
Ice bucket	$60-70
Parfait	$90-95
Pitcher, 64 oz.	$170-175
Plate, sherbet, 6.5"	$30-40
Plate, luncheon, 8.25"	$35-40
Relish, divided	$25-35
Salt and pepper	$65-100
Saucer	$30-40
Sherbet	$25-35
Sherbet, ruffled	$35-45
Tumbler, footed, 6 oz.	$35-45
Tumbler, footed, 5.25"	$35-40
Tumbler, footed, 11 oz.	$45-60
Tumbler, footed, 12 oz.	$60-75

Thumbprint

Made by the Federal Glass Company from 1927 to 1930.

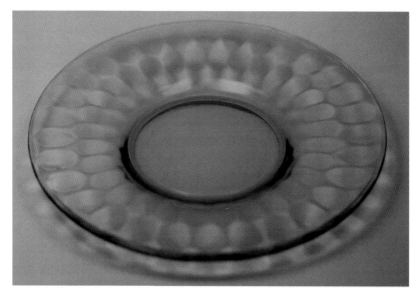

Bowl, berry, 4.75"	$10-15	Plate, dinner, 9.25"	$24-25
Bowl, cereal, 5"	$10-15	Salt and pepper	$65-80
Bowl, berry, 8"	$20-25	Saucer	$2-4
Creamer	$12-18	Sherbet	$9-10
Cup	$6-8	Sugar	$12-18
Plate, sherbet, 6"	$5-10	Tumbler, 5.5"	$10-30
Plate, luncheon, 8"	$7-15		

Twisted Optic

Made by the Imperial Glass Company from 1927 to 1930.

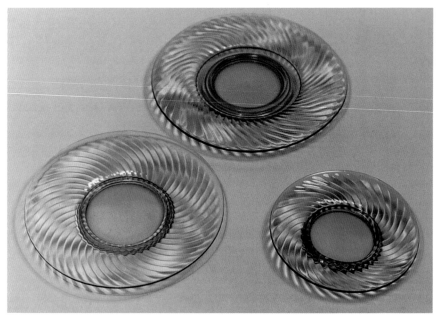

Basket	$40-45
Bowl, cream soup	$10-12
Bowl, cereal, 5"	$7-8
Bowl, salad, 7"	$10-12
Bowl, 9"	$17-18
Candy jar and cover	$35-45
Creamer	$9-12
Cup	$5-7
Mayonnaise	$18-20
Pitcher, 64 oz.	$35-40
Plate, sherbet, 6"	$2-4
Plate, salad, 7"	$3-6
Plate, luncheon, 8"	$3-7
Plate, sandwich, 10"	$3-12
Platter, oval with indent, 9" x 7.5"	$6-7
Sandwich server, center handle	$18-22
Sandwich server, two handles	$12-15
Saucer	$2-4
Sherbet	$7-10
Sugar	$6-12
Tumbler, 9 oz., 4.5"	$8-10
Tumbler, 12 oz., 5.25"	$10-12

Windsor ("Windsor Diamond")

Made by the Jeannette Glass Company from 1932 to 1946.

Bowl, berry, 4.75"	$10-12
Bowl, cream soup	$25-30
Bowl, deep cereal, 5.5"	$33-35
Bowl, with handles, 8"	$24-25
Bowl, large berry, 8.5"	$18-25
Bowl, oval vegetable, 9.5"	$29-30
Bowl, boat shape, 7" x 11.75"	$35-45
Butter dish	$95-100
Cake plate, 10.75"	$22-35
Creamer	$12-15
Cup	$12-22
Pitcher, 6.75"	$55-70
Plate, sherbet, 6"	$6-8
Plate, salad, 7"	$20-25
Plate, dinner, 9"	$25-35
Plate, chop, 13.62"	$40-42
Platter, oval, 11.5"	$25-30
Salt and pepper	$48-65
Saucer	$5-10
Sherbet	$15-20
Sugar and cover	$40-50
Tray, square, 4"	$12-15
Tray, with handles, 4.25" x 9"	$15-16
Tumbler, flat, 3.25"	$35-42
Tumbler, flat, 4"	$35-39
Tumbler, 4.5"	$55-60
Tumbler, 5"	$55-60

Chapter Three

Miscellaneous Items

Anchor Hocking Glass Company

Left. Fire King Jade-ite refrigerator box with crystal lid, 4" x 4". $20-22.
Right. Jade-ite refrigerator box with crystal lid, 4" x 8". $35-40.

Left. Jade-ite Shell round vegetable bowl, 8.5" in diameter, c. 1960s-1970s. $24-26.
Right. Jade-ite Shell saucer, 5.75" in diameter, c. 1960s-1970s. $6-8.

Left. Jade-ite Beaded Edge mixing bowl, 7.12". $12-14.
Center. Jade-ite Beaded Edge mixing bowl, 6". $10-12.
Right. Jade-ite Beaded Edge mixing bowl, 4.88". $17-20.

Jade-ite batter bowl with 1" band. $30-45.

Left. Jade-ite restaurant ware bowl, c. 1940s-1960s. $18-20.
Right. Jade-ite restaurant ware mug, c. 1940s-1960s. $20-22.

Left. Jade-ite Swirl mixing bowl, 8". $17-20.
Center. Jade-ite Swirl mixing bowl, 7". $15-17.
Right. Jade-ite Swirl mixing bowl, 5". $45-55.

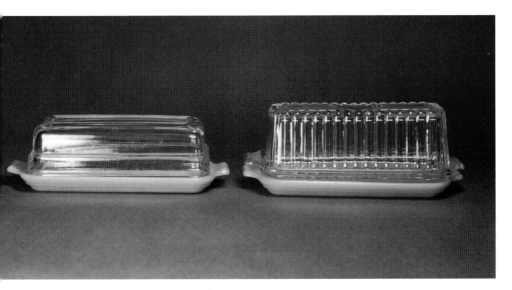

Left. Jade-ite butter dish with crystal lid. $67-70.
Right. Jade-ite ribbed butter dish with ribbed crystal lid. $80-90.

Left. Jade-ite batter bowl with 0.75" band. $25-30.
Right. Jade-ite batter bowl with 1" band. $30-35.

Jade-ite five compartment divided restaurant plate with cup, 9.63" plate, c. 1940s-1960s.
Plate: $37-40; cup: $10-12.

Jade-ite restaurant ware c. 1940s-1960s.
Left. Oval platter, 9.5". $54-57.
Center left. Mug, $10-12.
Center left. Fruit bowl, 4.74". $10-13.
Center right. Mug. $10-12.
Right. Oval platter, 11.5". $44-47.
Left back. three compartment restaurant ware plate, 9.63". $27-30.
Right back. five compartment restaurant ware plate, 9.63". $37-40.

Jade-ite restaurant ware mugs. $10-12 each.

Left. Forest green creamer. $10-12.
Right. Forest green sugar. $10-12.

Forest green Harding vase. $15-18.

Forest green pitcher, 86 oz. $38-47.

Left. Forest green ashtray, 4.62", c.1950-1965. $7-8.
Right. Forest green ashtray, 5.75", c.1953. $9-10.

Forest green juice glass. $5-6.

Bartlett-Collins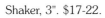

Shaker, 3". $17-22.

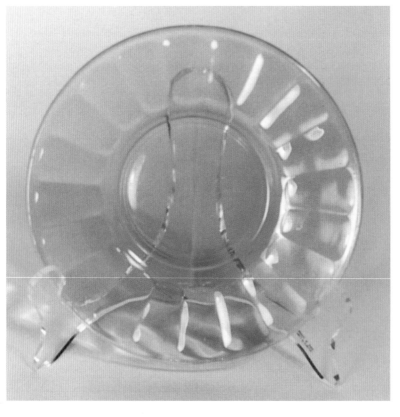

NuGreen plate,
8". $5-8.

NuGreen molasses can, 12 oz. with metal lid.
$50-65.

Left. "Twitch" cup and saucer. Cup: $4-6; saucer: $3-5.
Center. "Twitch" sherbet. $7-9.
Center back. "Twitch" tumbler. $6-8.
Right. "Twitch" pitcher. $40-45.

Federal Glass Company

Optic Paneled sherbet. $10-15 each.

Optic Paneled candy dish. $35-40.

Coaster with Diana characteristics. $8-12.

Federal Jr. sherbet. $7-10.

Optic Paneled cup and saucer. $10-12.

Greensburg Glass Works
whiskey glass, 1 oz.. $8-10.

Hazel-Atlas Glass Company

Salt and peppers. $10-25 each.

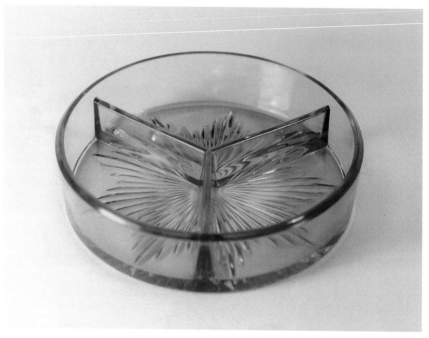

G-1155 5" three compartment candy tray. $12-18.

Left. Measuring cup. $15-20.
Right. 1 qt. 4 cup footed reamer pitcher. $30-35.

Refrigerator container. $20-22.

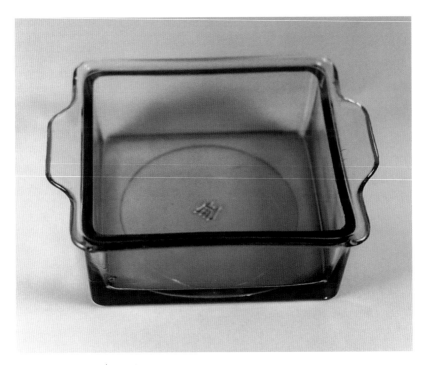

Refrigerator dish. $17-19.

Coasters. $5-7 each.

Tumblers. $8-12 each.

9 oz. table tumbler. $8-12.

G-3036 fruit cup, 3". $6-8.

Custard cup, 2.5". $6-8.

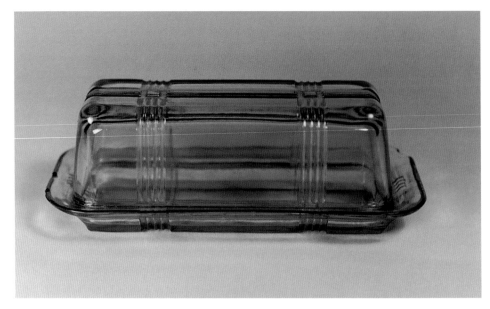

Crisscross butter dish. $20-25.

Reamer. $22-25.

Berry bowl with ruffled edge. $9-12.
Large berry bowl with ruffled edge. $39-35.

Hocking Glass Company

Left. Reamer. $10-12.
Center. Orange reamer. $12-15.
Right. Hazel-Atlas reamer. $12-15.

Pair of footed tumblers. $10-15 each.

Shakers. $18-25 each.

Left. Mixing bowl, 10.25". $18-20.
Right. Mixing bowl, 9.5". $15-18.

Orange reamer. $12-15.

Batter bowl, handled. $20-25.

130

Imperial Glass Company

Pair of fan shaped vases, 8". $18-25 each.

Twisted Optic tumbler. $9-12.

Bowl, $18-20.

Lindburgh cake plates. $35-45 each.

Pillar Flute salad plate, 8". $7-12.

Indiana Glass Company

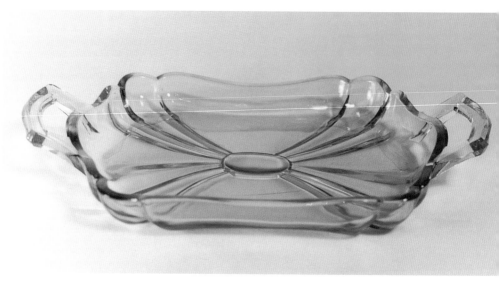

"Bananas" No. 611 pattern, 8" oblong tray. $45-55.

Jeanette Glass Company

Tumblers, 9 oz. $4-5 each.
Jug, 33 oz. $25-27.

McKee Glass Company

Plate for stemmed sherbet. $10-12.

Paden City Glass Manufacturing Company

Vases. $20-25 each.

L.E. Smith Glass Company

Pair of candy jars with covers. $25-45 each.

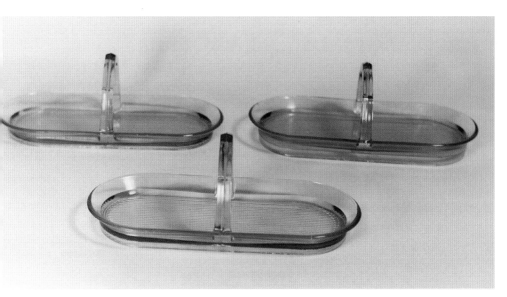

Trio of Greensburg celery dishes. $15-25 each.

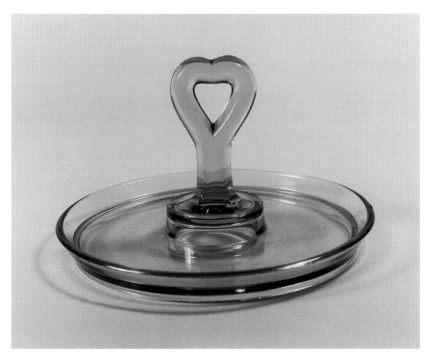

Greensburg handled beverage tray. $15-20.

Flower bowl. $20-25.

Left. Tumbler, 4.5". $7-10.
Right. Sherbet tray. $8-12.

Grill plate. $10-12.

U.S. Glass Company

Left. Octagon sugar. $10-15.
Right. Octagon creamer. $10-15.

Octagon luncheon plate. $10-12.
Octagon sandwich plate. $12-14.
Octagon cup. $6-7.
Octagon saucer. $4-6.

Bimbo mixing bowl, 4.5" deep and 8.5" in diameter. $30-35.

Slick plate, 9". $8-12.

Pitcher with lid from reamer pitcher set. Complete set is $250-275.

Pitcher. $25-30.

Shaggy Daisy bowl with three feet. $18-22.

Rose and Thorn bowl, 11". $18-22.

Side view of Rose and Thorn bowl, 11". $18-22.

Miscellaneous

Spoke "Wagon Wheel," maker unknown.
Left. Sherbet, footed. $4-5.
Left back. Tumbler. $4-6.
Center front. Plate. $7-9.
Center back. Bowl. $7-9.
Right. Bowl. $5-8.

Left. Ladle. $12-14.
Right. Mayonnaise. $15-18.

Cake plate, 10". $10-15.

146

Left. Mildred plate. $8-10.
Right. Mildred cup and saucer. $10-12.

Above. Sherbet. $8-10.
Right. Dessert plate. $9-12.

Assorted ashtrays. $8-12.

Flower bowl and block. $35-45.

"Kraft" cheese dish, green with crystal cover, 5" base. $44-48.

Nappy with block panel design, 4.5". $5-7.

Violet jar. $8-10.

Nappy. $4-6.

Butter tub. $10-15.

Sherbet. $6-9.

Diamond Panel bowl. $12-15.

Candy jar with cover, 8.5". $20-30.

Left. Tumbler. $8-10.
Center. Tumbler. $6-8.
Right. Sherbet. $5-7.

Assorted reamers. $12-20 each.

Inspiration – Burple tumbler. $8-10 each.
Inspiration – Burple sherbet. $7-9 each.

Anchor Hocking Boopie tumblers, 6 oz. $8-10 each.

Bibliography

Archer, Margaret and Douglas. *Imperial Glass.* Paducah, Kentucky: Collector Books, 1990.

Brenner, Robert. *Depression Glass for Collectors.* Atglen, Pennsylvania: Schiffer Publishing, Ltd., 1998.

Florence, Gene. *Pocket Guide to Depression Glass.* Paducah, Kentucky: Collector Books, 2001.

"The History of Anchor Hocking 1905-1906." http://www.anchorhocking.com.

Mauzy, Barbara and Jim Mauzy. *Mauzy's Comprehensive Handbook of Depression Glass Prices.* Atglen, Pennsylvania: Schiffer Publishing, Ltd., 2001.

Measell, James and Berry Wiggins. *Great American Glass of the Roaring 20s & Depression Era.* Marietta, Ohio: The Glass Press, Inc., 1998.

Schroy, Ellen T. *Warman's Depression Glass: A Value & Identification Guide.* Iola, Wisconsin: Krause Publications, 2000.

Weatherman, Hazel Marie. *Colored Glassware of the Depression Era.* Springfield, Missouri: Weatherman Glassbooks, 1970.

Weatherman, Hazel Marie. *Colored Glassware of the Depression Era 2.* Springfield, Missouri: Weatherman Glassbooks, 1974.

A Pocket Guide to Pink Depression Era Glass. Revised & Expanded 2nd Edition. Patricia Clements and Monica Clements. During the Great Depression, glass companies turned to machine-made methods to produce inexpensive, colorful glass. Due to its wonderful variety, availability, beauty, and usefulness, this type of glassware has endured to become one of the hottest collectibles on today's antiques market. This is the first book to extensively cover only Depression Era pink glass; pink was the most popular color of glassware then and has retained its popularity to the present day. It contains over 200 color photographs, examples of forty-five patterns, and brief histories of glass companies such as Bartlett-Collins, Cambridge, Federal, Fostoria, Hazel-Atlas, Imperial, Westmoreland, and others. This revised and expanded second edition features some new photographs and newly revised prices. It is an indispensable guide for all who collect Depression era glass and enjoy the beauty of pink glassware.

Size: 6" x 9"	232 color photos	160pp.
Price Guide		
ISBN: 0-7643-1369-X	soft cover	$16.95

Pocket Guide to Carnival Glass. Monica Lynn Clements & Patricia Rosser Clements. This attractive pocket guide presents the story of Carnival Glass, with a chapter giving an overview of how Carnival Glass has endured. Included are brief histories of Dugan, Fenton, Imperial, Millersburg, and Northwood. Over 200 beautiful color photographs will teach you how to identify classic Carnival Glass patterns as well as contemporary Carnival Glass pieces, along with the values you can expect to see in today's marketplace. For anyone who enjoys the beauty of the classic patterns or for those who appreciate the timeless appeal of more recent iridised glass, this book is a must.

Size: 6" x 9"	208 color photos	128pp.
Price Guide		
ISBN: 0-7643-1197-2	soft cover	$16.95

Forest Green Glass. Philip L. Hopper. This new book presents an important part of Anchor Hocking's glass production, the dark "Forest Green" styles made from the late 1950s through the mid-1960s. The history and variety of Forest Green glassware is precisely documented here, covering seventeen established patterns, many boxed sets, and a myriad of accessory pieces such as relish sets, ashtrays, lamps, vases, pitchers, and tumblers. These and many other styles are beautifully presented in over 300 gorgeous color photographs. Many pages of historical documentation are included to make this the most comprehensive reference guide to Anchor Hocking's Forest Green glassware.

Size: 8 1/2" x 11"   304 color photos   112pp.
Price Guide/Index
ISBN: 0-7643-1058-5   soft cover $19.95

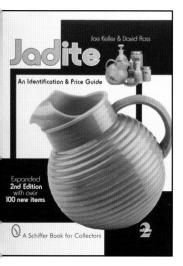

Jadite: An Identification and Price Guide. Revised & Expanded 2nd Edition. Joe Keller & David Ross. Many books have been written on Depression Era kitchenware and dinnerware, yet none have focused on the mass-produced opaque green glassware known as jadite. This book attempts to bring together the works of the three major glass companies that produced jadite: McKee, Jeannette, and Anchor Hocking. Produced from the early 1930s until the mid-1970s, jadite has rapidly become one of today's hottest collectibles. In addition to numerous dinnerware patterns, all sorts of jadite kitchenware was produced, including canisters, shakers, mixing bowls, and ovenware. Jadite items were also made for the rest of the home, including lamps, bathroom items, and ashtrays. The authors have produced a book which identifies over a thousand jadite pieces with more than 500 photos and current values.

Size: 8 1/2" x 11"   491 color photos   144pp.
Price Guide
ISBN: 0-7643-1091-7   hard cover $24.95

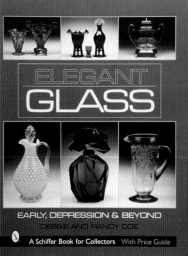